PowerShell

— — — — — ❧❧❧❧ — — — — —

Best Practices to Excel While Learning
PowerShell Programming

Miles Price

liable for any hardship or damages that may befall them after undertaking information described herein.

Additionally, the information in the following pages is intended only for informational purposes and should thus be thought of as universal. As befitting its nature, it is presented without assurance regarding its prolonged validity or interim quality. Trademarks are mentioned without written consent and can in no way be considered an endorsement from the trademark holder.

Table of Contents

Introduction

Congratulations on downloading PowerShell and thank you for doing so.

The following chapters will discuss how to quickly and efficiently become a solid PowerShell programmer without wasting any of your own time.

There are plenty of books on this subject on the market, so thanks again for choosing this one! Every effort was made to ensure it is full of as much useful information as possible, please enjoy!

Chapter 1:
Learning What PowerShell Is

So, before we do anything else, we need to try to gain some sort of understanding of what PowerShell is and what functionality it can offer you as the end user, as well as why you should start to use it in the first place.

The easiest way to explain PowerShell is to take a bit of a trip down memory lane. So, for just a moment, pretend that you aren't sitting in front of a modern computer right now, with its frilly user interface and all of the bells and whistles that you know it for. In fact, if you were to go back far enough, the computer would be very barebones and not as sleek.

Once upon a time, the only way to interact with a computer was through the use of what was known as 'command line interfaces.' These would allow you to access critical parts of the system, like the hard drive, and do things such as create and edit files, directories, and more. Moreover, these command line interfaces provided the primary method by which you would create, run, and generally *use* programs. These would continue to develop over a long period of time with the computer itself, growing in complexity as the computer which they ran on did.

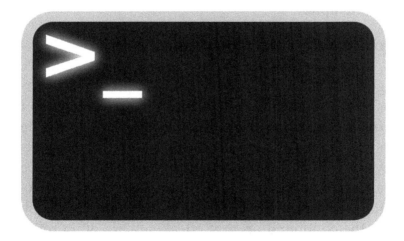

Many of these early command line interfaces would grow into the things which we are familiar with today. For example, MS-DOS and Unix started out as command line interface operating systems before eventually growing graphical user interfaces as the capabilities of computers grew.

PowerShell

As computers developed graphical user interfaces, however, the command line interface didn't fall by the wayside. The fact is that there are many processes that computers can carry out that are massively simplified or streamlined by the command line, that can be carried out without having to perform unnecessary clicks and moving between one window to another. The typical graphical user interface is based on what is called the 'desktop metaphor,' which is basically a reference to the fact that the computer's interface tries to mimic a literal desktop in the way you move from one task to another. This has natural limitations, such as the scope of your focus being limited to a set number of tasks at a time, as well as requiring you to navigate between things within the context of the desktop metaphor.

The command line interface doesn't suffer from this sort of issue. What once was MS-DOS would slowly become accessed through what is known as the command prompt on Windows, or cmd.exe. Through the command prompt, you can do things that you wouldn't be able to do normally through the desktop metaphor, often with more ease than you would otherwise. However, there is a counterpoint to this; you can be certain, for example, that there is a pretty large learning curve to using the command prompt. There is a reason that the people who can use the command prompt effectively are often referred to as 'power users.'

Anyhow, the question I have yet to really answer is how PowerShell relates to all of this. Well, PowerShell relates to it all in a very crucial way.

Think back to the operating system Unix that I mentioned a little bit earlier. For all intents and purposes, Unix is long dead and gone, having died out sometime in the late 1980s or early 1990s. However, one of the primary capabilities of Unix was the fact that its specific command line interface, commonly known as the 'Terminal,' offered quite a bit of power to the users who were behind the keyboard. So popular was Unix and its command line schema, in fact, that in its stead, many similar operating systems were born that attempted to emulate the Unix methodology.

These operating systems would come to be known as 'Unix-like.' Many of the operating systems that coexist alongside Windows today, such as the Linux operating systems, Mac OS X, and other common operating systems like FreeBSD, are intended in one way or another to at least emulate the Unix systems in terms of their core functionality, though they may be somewhat distended in terms of their aesthetics or even overall manner of processing.

One key feature that all of these operating systems would adapt from the Unix paradigm was the notion of a powerful command line interface. Many of these systems would develop their own forms of Terminals, carrying over Unix commands and the general Unix methodology for moving through the system using the command line interface.

Allow us to draw, at the same time, a parallel between this and for Windows. The first iteration of Windows to really hit the market was in the form discussed a bit previously, MS-DOS. MS-DOS also offered a very powerful command line navigation tool, but the exact usage of this tool varied a little bit from the Unix methodology. While some things remained similar, such as navigation through the system, core functionalities were often quite different.

Bearing that in mind, we must consider how Windows and Linux/Mac OS X would start to develop in different linear paths, with an essential focus on Linux since Mac OS X was able to find a niche market as a more professional operating system based around simplicity, where Linux and Windows were to become the more barebones workhorses of the tech world. Windows' second primary iteration came along in the form of an operating system called Windows 3.1. This was the first case in which Windows began to use and extend the desktop metaphor, creating a smash on the market with a relatively intuitive GUI and heavy support for business programs that was bolstered, somewhat, by Bill Gates' unethical business decisions.

As Windows would continue through various iterations, the focus would become that of ensuring that the system would be focused towards the user who needed to get something done and also a computer for the everyman, easily affordable and easy enough to navigate, the system would start to simplify a bit. The actions of the former MS-DOS would be consolidated to the command line or various different utilities scattered throughout the system.

In other words, a stark separation developed between the Windows command line and the experience of the average user of Windows, such that many people could get away with using Windows without ever really having to use a command line.

We should compare this, of course, to Linux systems, which were the primary torch-bearer for the Unix methodology. Linux became the system for power users, IT professionals, and those who simply wanted more control over their system. While it's impossible to really landmark things in Linux's history, given the nature of Linux as a core open-source kernel that other systems are built on top of, leading to the spawning of a legion of different operating systems that all perform functionally similarly at their core, the most popular Linux distributions such as Fedora, Debian, Ubuntu, and Linux Mint all show something rather clear. And that is: regardless of Linux's popularity, the same stark divide between power users and the everyday users of the system never seemed to occur.

Take, for example, the process of opening a file that requires permissions. In systems Windows 7 and more modern versions, you can right-click on the file and give it administrator rights so that it may make changes to your system.

On the other hand, compare this to the Ubuntu paradigm. The method by which you must modify the permissions of the system requires the usage of the command line in an essential manner. There isn't a way to circumvent this without acquiring additional software; the command line is deeply integrated into the workflow of the Ubuntu design and, similarly, most other Linux systems.

This sets up a dichotomy where Linux had over time become the system for power users. While the Windows command prompt was powerful, it didn't offer anywhere near the level of flexibility or utility that the Linux terminal did.

However, this came alongside another consideration for Microsoft: how does one go about creating more utility for power users while also keeping in consideration the fact that Windows itself is aimed at the everyman and not intended for somebody to study it extensively before it can be used?

The answer would eventually come along in the form of PowerShell. PowerShell started being developed sometime late into the product cycle of Windows Vista, finally seeing a full release during the product cycle of Windows 7. The PowerShell created a new paradigm that massively expanded upon the command prompt capabilities of Windows, but also enabled users, at last, to integrate the Windows command line workflow more intuitively into their everyday work.

So in essence, what is the PowerShell? Well, at face value, it's simply a command prompt, but there's a whole lot more to it than that.

Thanks to things like PowerShell, you will be able to automate many processes that otherwise would be difficult to automate through the usage of stuff such as the pipeline and user-created scripts. Moreover, thanks to PowerShell, you will be able to get access to information on your computer that you couldn't previously and perform basic tasks like connecting via networks to other computers that are difficult to perform without having a utility like PowerShell ready to do it for you.

Almost every user can benefit from the knowledge of how to use PowerShell, but people who aspire to use their computer at a higher level of knowledge — for example, the programmers, the system administrators, and the network administrators — will find themselves very happy to have a utility like PowerShell at their disposal.

One reason that programmers will find PowerShell incredibly useful is its design choices. One principle thing about PowerShell is that it was designed from the ground up to integrate cleanly with other things in the Microsoft .NET suite.

This is partially a reflection by Microsoft intended to make Windows and PowerShell an appealing alternative for people who aspire to be power users. However, on the other hand, it also is a reflection of the fact that the .NET suite is growing massively. For example, the language C# — a language developed for use on Microsoft products through the .NET suite — has seen a very quickly growing presence in the business world since its release. Languages like F# in the .NET suite are growing as well, geared towards those in data science.

PowerShell

So, in the end, the presence of PowerShell is growing a lot, and the integration of PowerShell seamlessly into the .NET suite is a function of the fact that it has gained so much dominance.

Chapter 2:
Setting Up PowerShell

Now that you've procured and installed PowerShell, one of the things that we need to focus on first is learning the commands. As I've said before, learning the command line is something which takes time and practice. However, it's not a monolithic task that will require all of your efforts. Fortunately, learning the command line is actually rather intuitive and comes without too much difficulty once you understand the structure.

With that said, it's important that we talk a bit about the structure of the command line and how it works, especially within the context of PowerShell.

One of the greatest things about PowerShell is that it offers full-fledged command over your PC. It does so through the use of commands. However, these differ from other commands in other shells because they are actually what are called cmdlets. Cmdlets differ a little bit in their mechanism of action from commands in other shells in a couple ways; the first of which is that they are a bit more versatile because of their integration with the other .NET framework entities. We'll go more into detail about those a bit later.

Anyhow, the other way that these differ from commands in other shells is that they actually take multiple forms. Within the PowerShell context, cmdlets have their initial form, known as the cmdlet itself. However, they also take on aliases.

Aliases act functionally the same as command lines do. The main purpose that they serve is to offer an easy point of convergence for people who are coming from either the old Windows command line shell or people who are coming from a Unix or Unix-like background. Indeed, many of the commands that are within PowerShell have been adapted from Unix counterparts or perform an old Windows functionality that is basically the same as the Unix alternative.

It is for this reason, too, that in describing these commands to you, I am going to be giving their aliases as well. The primary purpose of this is to take the knowledge that you gain in this chapter and attempt to make it portable, meaning that no matter what command line you go to, you're going to have a decent enough time to work your way around the shell. For example, thanks to the knowledge that you gain in this book, you'll have an easy enough time writing Bash scripts for Linux should you ever need to.

Command line shells often act in similar ways. This means that we can distill a lot of their actions into commonalities. For example, on one hand, you always have the core concept: the 'command.' However, commands can also accept information. When a command accepts information, it is called an 'argument.' Different commands will accept different arguments, and some may not accept any. Arguments can massively change the output or the mechanism through which the command performs. Essentially, arguments give you the ability to actually do things with the programs rather than having the programs perform a single action.

The general structure of a command line statement is as such:

command/cmdlet arguments

You may also notice from time to time that these are separated by a pipe (|). This introduces the concept known as a pipeline. Prior to PowerShell, Windows didn't really have a pipeline concept. It was with PowerShell that Windows finally forayed more extensively into the world of command line usability.

So what is the pipeline? The pipeline is an essential idea in understanding how and why certain commands work, as well as how the command line in general works. The pipeline is best visualized by thinking of an actual pipeline. It's a reference to the mechanism by which information is obtained and relayed in the computer.

On one end of the pipe, you have the user input. This is the command that you enter to perform some given action. On the other end of the pipe, you have the program output. This what the command line eventually spits back at you after parsing the information that you sent to it in the first place.

Between this, though, you may need to perform certain operations. The concept of the pipeline enables you to chain multiple of these input and output pipes together using, appropriately, the pipe character.

Let's say that you had the following structure:

command1 | command2

Imagine this as two separate pipes: you have the command1 pipe and the command2 pipe. The command1 pipe initiates when you call it. It doesn't necessarily have to have input. The start of the pipe can rather be seen as the point at which the given action begins.

The end of the pipe then comes, which is, in effect, the point at which you are given information from command1.

Now, visualize the command2 pipe; it would be much the same. It is instantiated by merely existing, accepting arguments as input if it is given any arguments. It also relays information as the method by which it comes to a close.

But what if you wanted to relay the information that command1 gives in such a way that it isn't printed out for you but rather given to command2 as an argument? Through the pipeline system, you can actually make this happen. This can spare you from, for example, having to export the data from command1 into a file that you can read into command2 or any other line of various illogical things.

This is also where one of the perks of being a command line power user starts to come up: the raw versatility of this sort of system. Imagine trying to perform this sort of operation through the desktop metaphor. You would first launch command1 as its own program. Then you would try to find some sort of way to store the information that it gave you. Afterward, you'd have to navigate to command2 as a separate program and then do whatever set of tasks were required for you to import the information from command1 into command2.

In the end, what results is a very unwieldy process that is massively simplified by the intuition of the command line: command1 | command2.

Anyway, the point of all of this is to give you some sort of idea as to how the command line works. There are a few other basic points that we need to cover, but we'll see where we are after we get through the cmdlets. For right now, we're just going to go through a bunch of basic cmdlets that you will need to be a PowerShell power user. Do note that this is far from an extensive list. Thanks to the nature of cmdlets, they are virtually endless, and you won't really ever see a list of them come to an end. However, this is the starting point that you need to really get started working with your computer on a greater level.

Get-ChildItem

Also known as *gci*, *dir*, or *ls*; all aliases work.

This command's name doesn't quite make sense if you don't really try to consider it from a computer science perspective.

However, if you've ever even touched another command line, then you have an acutely aware idea of what this command's purpose is thanks to its aliases. What this command basically does is just takes into consideration your location on the hard drive then uses that to list every file and directory within your location.

Test-Connection

Known in other shells as *ping*, but it doesn't have an alias in PowerShell.

This command is immensely important, so it's rather bizarre that it didn't carry over the only name it has ever really taken as an alias. Anyhow, the point of this command is that when given a certain address, it will attempt to establish a connection between you and the said computer. This connection may be over the internet or some other connection. It doesn't quite matter, as its very purpose is just to tell you whether you two are connected.

Get-Content

Also known as *gc*, *type*, or *cat*; all aliases work.

This command is one with a very straightforward name. The primary purpose for it is to be used in pipelines as a method of giving information from one command to another command. It allows you to obtain the information from a given file so that you may do something with it.

Get-Command

Also known as *gcm*.

This command is immensely useful given the intense breadth of different commands and *cmdlets* available to you in PowerShell. If you were to enter it, you would be fed back an immense list of *cmdlets*. The neat part is that all of these perform a different function, many of them are very capable and with a lot of functions under the hood. In essence, this is the gateway between you and automation of a large amount of your work experience on your computer. You can definitely speed things up quite a bit using the Get-Command *cmdlet*.

Get-Help

Also known as help, apropos, or man. It may be called using aliases help and man on PowerShell.

This command will be of immense value to you, especially when you pair it with commands given to you by the previous command. The thing about this specific command is that it must take an argument, in the form of another command. Let's say, for example, that you wanted to better understand how the Test-Connection *commandlet* works. What you would do is enter the following:

Get-Help Test-Connection

This would print the following:

NAME

Test-Connection

SYNTAX

Test-Connection [-ComputerName] <string[]> [-AsJob] [-DcomAuthentication {Default | None | Connect | Call | Packet

| PacketIntegrity | PacketPrivacy | Unchanged}] [-WsmanAuthentication {Default | Basic | Negotiate | CredSSP | [...]

The output was shortened for brevity, but it will print out all of the information that the computer has on deck for that specific command, and give you a rather detailed idea of how the command can be used as well as how it should be entered into the console in terms of arguments.

Clear-Host

Also known as *cls* or *clear*; all aliases work.

This is another case of a basic *cmdlet* having a rather unwieldy name that does more harm than good unless you have a bit of a background in computer science; however, all that this command really does is clear the terminal of any text that is currently on it so that you have a blank screen to work with.

Copy-Item

Also known as *copy* or *cp*. Both aliases work, as well as *cpi*.

This command has a lot of utility behind it, especially in writing things such as install scripts, should you ever need to do such a thing. What it essentially does is allows you to designate a certain file or directory as an argument. You then designate a given target directory. Upon execution, the file or directory named in the first argument will be copied over to the given target directory. The efficiency of this command doesn't just stop at install scripts, though; it can also be highly useful for doing stuff like making backup procedures.

Move-Item

Also known as *move* and *mv*; all aliases work.

This command, you'll find, is rather similar to the Copy-Item command. The primary difference is that instead of creating a carbon copy of files in a given target location, it will copy the files and then delete them in their original location, effectively moving them from one location to another.

Remove-Item

Also known as *del*, *erase*, *rmdir*, and *rd*; all aliases work, as well as *ri*.

Allow me to start by saying that this command is dangerous. It has a lot of different names, and it can be of great use to you. However, it is also an insanely powerful command and failing to take proper care in using it can actually lend itself to you doing something like wiping your whole hard drive clean.

There's no way to recover from something like that. If you find yourself really wanting to practice this command — as I said, it can be quite useful to know how it works — then you should likely do so within a Terminal inside a Linux virtual machine, or a PowerShell installation in a Windows virtual machine. If you mess up the command within these contexts, then the damage done is rather minimal as it's detached from your primary operating system installation on your local hard drive. What this command basically does is remove a target item or directory from the hard drive and completely deletes it, meaning that there isn't a very easy recovery method for items deleted through this method. There are certain ways to call this *cmdlet* that can very easily wipe your hard drive, so be careful and get practice with the command before you even try using it.

Rename-Item

Also known as *mi*, *ren*, and *mv*.

This command does pretty much what the name implies. You can specify a target file or directory as an argument and then specify what you'd like to rename it to. There's not much more to say about it; it's simple and straightforward.

Get-Location

Also known as *cd* or *pwd*. Both aliases work, as well as *gl*.

This command is useful when you're in the middle of your workflow because it will allow you to see what working directory you are currently in. In case you didn't know, the working directory is an important term in command line programming that simply refers to whatever directory you are currently within in the context of your command line shell.

Push-Location

Also known as *pushd*; this is the only alias available on PowerShell.

This command works similarly to other directory commands in this list, but it has a bit more of a tricky explanation than the other commands listed here. This is because it requires you to understand the introductory computer science concept of a 'stack.' The stack is a fundamental lesson in computer science; it allows you to store data in an efficient and easily accessible way. Think of it in terms of an actual stack. If you were to have a stack of objects, then you could put something new on top of the stack. However, then, the new object on the very top of the stack is whatever it is that you put on there. If you want to get to something lower in the stack, then, you'll have to remove items sequentially until you get there. In essence, stacks allow you to retrieve data as needed, but they also put a limitation in the name of efficiency, you can only draw data from the thing on the very top of the stack. The Push-Location *cmdlet* allows you to add a new directory to the top of the stack. When you recall this location later, you will be instantly taken to that location.

Pop-Location

Also known as *popd*; this is the only alias available on PowerShell.

Pop-Location performs the inverse operation of Push-Location in that it allows you to go to the directory on the very top of the stack. Once you go there, the value will be removed from the stack. Bear in mind that if you want to have the directory in the stack again, it will no longer be there, so you'll have to add it using Push-Location again. In essence, remember: you push values onto the stack, then you pop them off of the stack. Using the combination of Push-Location and Pop-Location, you can jump around your hard drive at ease moving from one location to another seamlessly. It will take practice, but if you are moving around your hard drive often, this utility can be a fantastic addition to your repertoire.

Set-Location

Also known as *cd* and *chdir*. Both aliases work, as well as *sl*.

There is definitely no command that is more fundamentally important to your studies than this one. This command allows you to easily move from one directory or another. The gist of this location is that it allows you to set your working directory to a certain place, therefore allowing you to navigate from one folder to another. You can use this command in a few different ways. One way is to enter the directory address of a specific location on your hard drive, which will jump from your working directory to that location. Additionally, you can just name a directory within the directory you're in (e.g., Set-Location Desktop if you're currently in C:/Users/name). You can also use '..' as your argument to move up a directory.

Tee-Object

Also known as *tee*.

This command can be rather useful, especially for printing out error logs and then processing the given error. However, there are many other situations where you may use this, and its usage will really depend upon a bunch of various factors. It will become clear when the time comes. For now, a cursory understanding of this command should do, as it is rather a niche. The Tee-Object command works in such a way that it takes a given input, and then it exports that to a file or value. After doing that, it will send it along the pipeline, whether that just means printing the data out to your console window or whether it means sending it to the next command in the pipeline.

Write-Output

Also known as *write*.

There are few commands with so straightforward a name as this one. Everything that you need to know about it is indicated heavily in its name. Write-Output will allow you to simply write to the output stream, whatever that may be, though it generally is the command line window. You will find this of exceptional importance when you start working with PowerShell scripting in the following chapters.

Get-Process

Also known as *ps* or *tasklist*; Both aliases work, as well as *gps*.

Get-Process is an important command because it is very functionally similar to something that a lot of people do on Windows systems all of the time. When you open the Task Manager using the 'Ctrl-Alt-Delete' sequence, you open a task manager that allows you to view whatever processes are running. This command allows you to take this process and move it to the command line. Used alone, it will print them out to the command line window. Used in tandem with other commands, it will send the information about the running processes onward so that you may work with them through other commands.

Stop-Process

Also known as *kill*; alias works, as well as *spps*.

The Stop-Process command pairs particularly well with the Get-Process command. It allows you to take any given process that is listed on the Get-Process menu and bring it to a grinding halt. This can be particularly useful when your computer is what most people in the IT field would refer to as 'stupid.' Let's say that you're trying to launch one program that requires access to a certain port, such as Skype, but another process is already blocking that port. Through Get-Process and a process query, you can discover what processes are using what ports; you can then bring whatever process is blocking your port to a stop. It's a very simple process.

Select-String

Also known as *sls*.

This process allows you to get the strings that are present in either a given file or a given input stream (such as the output from the last thing in the pipeline). If you aren't yet familiar with strings in a conceptual sense, then don't worry; we'll be covering that in the chapter regarding programming logic. Bear in mind that it returns the whole line that a string is on, so if you were to do a Select-String for the term 'ack' in a file full of different words, then it would return 'black,' 'crack,' 'smack,' and 'attack.' This command is easy to use and quite powerful.

Set-Variable

Also known as *sv* and *set*; both aliases work.

This command will allow you to create new variables and then give them a certain value, or change the value saved to an existing variable. It's straightforward. There are more concepts that we will cover in the chapters following, so no worries.

Get-Member

No aliases available.

This is one more command that is particularly useful to you as a potential PowerShell scripter. It has no known aliases because there isn't a parallel in other command line shells. This is yet another case where the mumbo-jumbo I'm about to throw at you won't make sense just yet, but again, it will. For now, just understand that this *cmdlet* will allow you to look at any given object and see the methods and values that are contained within that given object. You will need this as time goes on, so try to remember it.

Invoke-WebRequest

Also known as *curl* and *wget*; both aliases work, as well as *iwr*.

This is a terribly important command to remember because it allows you to pull data from the internet. If you have any experience with Linux command lines, then you're probably familiar with this one as it is often used to download things from the Internet and, aside from package managers, offers the primary way of downloading new things on most Unix-like systems.

Chapter 3:
Learning the Programming Logic

Now that you have a bit of a grasp on the different commands and *cmdlets* that you can use in the context of PowerShell, it's time that we start to talk a bit more about the underlying programming logic of PowerShell.

See, one of the key things that you need to understand about PowerShell is that one of the main draws of PowerShell isn't just in that it makes the command line on Windows powerful enough to be competitive with the Unix-inspired terminal. While that is a factor, it actually excels in one major factor: PowerShell actually has a full scripting language that comes alongside it and that integrates extremely well into it.

What I mean by this is that in comparison to other scripting languages specifically designed for programming and writing scripts, like Python, Perl, or Lua, PowerShell's language actually doesn't fall short.

The major reason for this incredible amount of power comes down to the fact that PowerShell fits together like a jigsaw puzzle piece with the rest of the .NET framework. At this point, that goes without saying. However, this kind of statement actually opens up another major question: Can we surely say that PowerShell and .NET are tightly integrated, but what on earth does this exactly mean?

In short, the first thing that you need to understand is that everything in PowerShell is an object. This is what makes the *cmdlets* in PowerShell different from commands on something like a Unix terminal or even the old Windows command line shell.

What an object is, in simple terms, is something that is derived from a class or namespace. But in layman's terms, the definition of an object becomes quite a bit more obtuse.

Within the context of computer science, we can develop a better definition of a 'class,' a class is a way of grouping different things together so that you can always create something that shares the same attributes. Imagine, for example, a dog. Every dog has four legs (barring unfortunate accidents, of course), a tail, ears, a fur color, a specific breed, and so forth. By broadly categorizing something as a dog, you're able to group all of these attributes together so that every dog is assumed to have these qualities. In this case, dog is the class. If you were to build on top of this, you could also say that every individual dog is an object of the dog class or an instance of the class.

Another thing that you need to understand is the key concept of a 'method.' A method is a block of code which carries out a specific action. It may or may not give a value back to you along the way. An example of a function would be if a dog barked. All dogs bark and bark could be seen as an action to be carried out:

Dog myDog

myDog.bark()

The second line would be a reference to the bark method, which would imply that the dog object 'myDog' is to bark.

The bottom line is that the PowerShell paradigm is heavily dependent upon methods. Methods are an important and absolutely critical part of working within PowerShell. Every *cmdlet* is an object instance of a greater command class, and because of this, they also have methods which are intrinsically connected to them as objects.

Along with this same line of logic, within PowerShell scripting, you can also create new objects. These custom objects are allowed to have values and methods which you personally define, which is a feature of high-level programming languages like Python and Java that carried over to PowerShell programming.

So, in the end, why does any of this matter? These things ultimately matter because these methods in PowerShell enable you to do a lot of things that you wouldn't be able to do otherwise. For example, these methods allow you to gain insight about the cmdlets that you're working with beyond what can be provided to you by the Get-Help command. Moreover, they also allow you to manipulate the data provided by the various cmdlets and other similar things.

In the end, methods are what gives PowerShell and *cmdlets* their, well, power.

The final key point of this chapter is that all objects are unique and that it is their specific attributes and methods which define them as objects. Just because two things of the same class are of the same class does not mean that they are at all the same. To move back to the dog example, consider for a second that there were two instances of the dog class, 'myDog1,' and 'myDog2.' The class 'myDog1' could have 4 legs, 2 ears, a tail, brown fur, and be a dachshund. Meanwhile, 'myDog2' could have 4 legs, 2 ears, a tail, brown fur, and be a terrier. Despite the fact that every other attribute is the same, the fact that the breed is different means that these are very clearly two different dogs. If we were to define more attributes, like their size or their name, there would just be even more distinguishing factors between these two objects. It is these intrinsic properties that simultaneously relate, define, and separate these two objects in an essential manner.

In other words, the properties of objects, especially of *cmdlets*, matter. Therefore, it's important that you understand that the properties and attributes are the things which make them unique despite the fact that they're all related in the sense of being an object of a greater class, and understanding this fact allows you to also understand the necessity of being able to access all of this information.

Chapter 4:
Learning How to Write and
Execute Scripts

In this chapter, we're going to finally start covering how you can begin automating numerous different processes in your workflow by using the PowerShell. PowerShell automation is achieved through writing scripts that you can execute (or execute by way of yet another script) that will carry out certain commands from within PowerShell for you.

In this chapter, we are also going to break down a lot of key programming concepts. This is because PowerShell is built on the .NET framework and, likewise, essentially is a programming language in and of itself. This means that many of the key concepts that apply to other programming languages will carry over to PowerShell without a problem.

This chapter will make the (potentially bold) assumption that you aren't a very experienced programmer and have little to no background in both programming and PowerShell. As such, when we come upon new concepts, we're going to take a minute to expand upon them and be sure that you understand them. Using the content in this chapter, you can start to really expand your knowledge of programming and PowerShell alike so long as you understand the underlying concepts.

So, what exactly is the point of writing scripts? There are two primary purposes. The first purpose is that you can, as I've said multiple times, automate things. Automation of certain processes can simplify things and take the strain out of an otherwise hectic computing process. More than that, you can also do things in a slightly different method than you would be able to if you just opened up PowerShell and started typing into it. For example, the usage of variables can open up the possibilities which are available to you rather widely.

You can generally write scripts for most command line shells. However, PowerShell scripts differ quite a bit from traditional command line shell scripts, such as 'Bash' scripts. For example, more traditional command-line scripts, you very well may have a set of certain commands that are written within the script, but they generally are very much the same as what you would just type straight into the console to get certain outputs. There are certain words, for sure, to direct program flow — things like basic if/else statements (we'll talk about these in a statement), GOTO statements, and barebones variables — but things to a bigger extent than this simply don't exist. Most command line shell scripting languages simply aren't that sophisticated.

However, the PowerShell language drives a hard parallel to this. While the PowerShell language certainly isn't as sophisticated as a language such as, say, Python or C++ — which can have dozens or even hundreds of different keywords — it is no less powerful than these languages for the most parts, and it manages to accomplish quite a bit and offer a lot of functionality despite offering only just about 24 keywords in total.

The lack of keywords doesn't make it any less powerful, just be aware. While it's not as sophisticated as a full-fledged programming language, it's far more sophisticated than things such as Bash scripting in terms of power and capability. To this end, it will be more than capable of doing anything that you really need it to do in terms of automation and writing console applications. The point of this chapter is to help you to harness the true ability of all of these different nuances within the programming language.

Let's start with the very basics: How does one create and run a given PowerShell script? Well, it all starts with a text editor. Inside the text editor, you just put in whatever your code is then you save it however you want to. The only thing to bear in mind during this whole process is that the name of the file has to end with *.ps1*, or in other words, the extension must be *ps1*. Therefore, if you wanted to have a script named 'rutabagas,' you would just name it as 'rutabagas.ps1.' Nothing more or less to it.

In terms of text editors that you can use, there are a lot of possibilities. Anything that can edit and create plaintext files is absolutely fine. I personally would recommend that you use Atom.io. There are many reasons for this, not the least of which is that Atom.io is free. It's entirely free, in fact, and you won't be paying for any part of it at any point in time, which is really impressive compared to competitive software such as Sublime Text. More than that, it's extensible, which means that there are a ton of add-ons that you can get for it and install to simplify your workflow. It's also a very beautiful and wonderful text editor with excellent syntax highlighting and easy to understand design cues.

Another great option would be something along the lines of Visual Studio Code. Visual Studio Code is designed to be lightweight and work easily and natively with Microsoft file types, as well as any other file types that you may end up needing to write, edit, or use.

On top of these two, there are other classics like Vim, Emacs, and Notepad++, alongside myriad other text editors that you can start learning and get used to. The choice ultimately comes down to whatever you are most comfortable with. As I said, the most important thing is that the editor can generate plaintext files.

With that out of the way, we're going to start breaking down different components of scripting logic and just start diving right in by writing our first script. Whatever your text editor is, open it up and then write the following line:

Write-Output "testing the script"

When that's done, go ahead and save the file as 'test.ps1' wherever you want. After that, you have two routes that you can take. The first is to simply navigate to the location in your File Explorer, right-click the file, and choose the option 'run with PowerShell.' However, you can also take the route which is considered far better practice and which will actually yield far better ends for you.

To do this, what you have to do is open your Start Menu. In the search box, type in '*PowerShell ISE.*' When the results pop up, right click on the 32-bit version (PowerShell ISE (x86)) and then click '*Run as Administrator.*' Now, if you're used to the usual PowerShell accessed by simply typing PowerShell, you'll notice immediately that this window is bigger, has a greater number of options, and also has a panel to one side brimming with info. From here, you just type the following into the window:

Set-ExecutionPolicy RemoteSigned

Once you've typed it, execute the command by pressing enter. What this does is that it allows your user account to execute PowerShell scripts from a command line without having to authorize it as an administrator every time. This will be important down the line when you're writing bigger scripts that need greater permission sets. It also allows you to chain scripts together from within PowerShell scripts, should you ever desire to do so.

Moving from this, what you're going to do next is navigate to the directory where you saved your script from within PowerShell. In the chapter concerning commands, we briefly talked about how one would do this. You do so essentially by utilizing the cd commands to move from place to place. If you need to know what folders are in your working directory, all that you do is use the *ls* alias to prompt the Get-ChildItem command. Navigate through the file system until you locate the file you made earlier.

From here, all that you're going to do to execute the file is the following:

./*test*.ps1

If you press Enter, then the script will run. After that, you'll see the console print out a testing script. From there, the script is done and you can now execute something else from within the PowerShell.

This is great progress, you've written your first script! Be proud, my friend.

With that out of the way, we need to start talking about the concepts that allow you to actually start automating things.

One of these core concepts is known as values and variables. These are an extremely important foundation of scripting and programming in general.

So what exactly is a value? A value is simultaneously easy and difficult to define in any meaningful context. On one hand, they're easy to understand. Values are generally just a way of referring to some sort of data.

As you know from things in real life, like when you discuss the value of a car or a home, you are discussing the monetary number which is attached to something. Moreover, value can reflect a specific quality.

It is following this line of logic that we're able to create a rather abstract definition of a value: data. Different values can be of different types of data, but all data is a form of value.

PowerShell programming allows for numerous different types of values. Here are just a few of the most popular that you are most likely to use in your programming ventures:

- **Array**

The array is a difficult type of value to describe; it's actually a value in and of itself, but also a set of other values that are combined and presented together.

- **Bool**

The term Bool refers to 'boolean,' which denotes what is simply a true or false value. Something can be one or the other. Truth and falsehood are heavily used in more spirited and crucial concepts such as conditional statements which we'll be talking about in a moment.

- **DateTime**

The DateTime value type is rather self-explanatory; it simply refers to an information format that contains a given date and time.

- **Float**

The Float data type stores a decimal number. This is the easiest way to remember it, anyway. There is a little bit more under the hood, but at the surface, it is simply a decimal number, or what is known in the comp sci sphere as a floating point number.

- **Guid**

This sort of value is actually relatively unique to PowerShell programming. It references a "globally unique ID," which are often affixed to different members of the global system to keep them clearly delineated.

- **HashTable**

If you have any sort of familiarity with languages such as Java, C++, and Python, then you are relatively familiar already with the concept of dictionaries. This carries over to PowerShell in the form of HashTables. HashTables store keys which connect to values. All of the keys link to one and exactly one value.

- **Integers**

The term integers mean the same thing that it means in mathematics: whole numbers.

- **PsObject**

PsObject is a value type which refers specifically to developed constructed PowerShell objects.

- **Regex**

This value type can store a regular expression. Chances are that you don't exactly know what a regular expression is; in short, a regular expression is a method of text parsing that allows the developer to keenly and exactly state precisely what they're looking for in a certain set of strings or characters.

- **String**

This value type is immensely important. It refers to a type of data wherein several different ASCII characters are linked together into a phrase, sentence, or any other form of textual data. ('1a35ce%,' 'math is fun,' and '!!!!!!' are all strings because they are all sets of ASCII characters linked together.)

Values can be stored within programming constructs known as 'variables.' Variables are basically boxes that hold certain values. Later, you can go and change the thing inside the box, or in some languages even get rid of the box altogether. This allows you to keep some value to be reused over and over under a certain name that you give it, which spares you the pain of having to retype something over and over.

Variables also allow your values to be dynamic because they prevent you from being required to hardcode everything. What this means is that since you aren't personally putting in every piece of information in the program, variables allow you to take in data from other sources than just yourself and then keep and manipulate them if needed.

Long ago, when programming languages were harder than they are now, you would generally have to explicitly say both the name of the variable and the type of the value that it's storing. You also would have to specify the type of the value that every method had. We'll be discussing methods more in-depth in a second, for the record.

Modern scripting languages like PowerShell, though, will often exempt you from the peril of having to type all of your variables. This is a blessing and a curse. Not having to specify the data type of your variables is known as 'implicit typing,' where requiring that the data type is specified is known as 'explicit typing.' Implicit typing can be a godsend in terms of readable and clear code, but on the other hand, it also can create quite a bit of confusion if you don't have a clear understanding on what the data types actually are if you ever have to do something like a variable cast.

Anyway, to set up a linkage between a variable and a value, you have to do what's called 'declaring a variable.'

Storing variables in PowerShell is a little bit similar to declaring variables in languages like PHP. Regardless of the type of variable that you're storing, all that you need to do to set up a variable with a value inside it is to just use a dollar sign alongside the variable's name. The variable's name can effectively be anything. There can even be spaces in the name if you put brackets around the name. With that said, good coding practices would indicate that you should not do that. Anyway, you have your dollar sign and your variable name. You follow this with an equal assignment operator (=) which tells the computer that the thing before the equals sign will assume the value of the thing after the equals sign.

For example, let's say we wanted to create a variable called 'myName' that stored the value, Jeff. We'd create this variable like so:

$myName = 'Jeff'

So, to explain what we just did, essentially we created a variable that can store the value type 'string.' We created this variable as a box specifically designed to hold this kind of value. That means that you can change the value within the variable the same way that you initialized it, but you have to be sure that it remains the same essential type of value.

Anyhow, within the string-shaped box that we created, we are now storing the value 'Jeff'. Easy, peasy.

Now that we've done this, we can now combine the two concepts that we've talked about — variables and output — into the same file. Let's make a new file, naming it whatever you want, and type the following inside:

$myName = 'Jeff'

Write-Output "Is your name $myName?"

If you then save this file, navigate to it in PowerShell, and try to run it the same way that you ran the last one, using './' to execute the file, then you should see it print out "Is your name Jeff?" to the console. With this, you have now created a variable and even manipulated it to prepare it for output.

Before we move onto the next section which involves the usage of math in PowerShell scripting, I feel I should make it clear. When you're printing out strings or saving them as a variable, you should ideally use single quotes around the string. The exception is if the string contains a variable; in these cases, you should use double quotes.

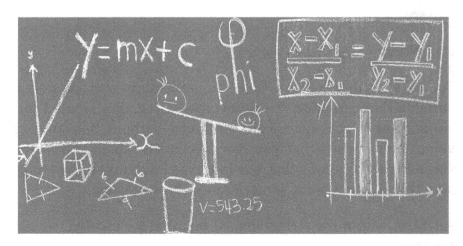

With that done, the next thing we're going to start discussing is math in the context of PowerShell. The first thing that we're going to do is define a few different variables in a new file:

$one = 2

$two = 3

The next thing that we're going to want to do is to create yet another variable, which we'll call — would you believe it? — three. We're going to assign this variable the addition of '$one' and '$two':

$three = $one + $two

From here, what we're going to do is write the following:

Write-Output "$one + $two = $three"

If you were to save this and then navigate to and run the file in PowerShell, it would print (hopefully):

2 + 3 = 5

This is great because it does a few things: first, it allows you to see how you can manipulate variables using other variables. Hopefully, this will solidify some sort of idea as to the function that variables and values actually perform in the context of a given program. It ideally should drive home the point that values truly are just data that you can work with and manipulate according to your needs.

It also gives you the opportunity to see PowerShell math at work. PowerShell math is based on operators that are used to carry out mathematical, well, operations. Here are the basic operators:

- +

Adds two values together.

- -

Subtracts the right value from left value.

- *

Multiplies two values together.

- /

Divides left value by right value.

- **-integer**

Before a number indicates that it is negative.

- %

Referred to as the 'modulo,' gives the remainder of a given division. For example, '5 % 2' would return 1 since the remainder of 5 / 2 is 1.

There are also iterative operators, like these:

- ++

Indicates "x = x + 1"; increases value by 1.

- --

Indicates "x = x - 1"; decreases value by 1.

Another thing that we need to talk about is control flow. Control flow is a lot more enjoyable of a topic to cover than variable manipulation and math operators, trust me. The notion of control flow is that it's the driver which will allow your program to make decisions. While you can easily write linear programs that carry out certain tasks and do this or that, it is through control flow that you can make your program have different outcomes based upon any variables that might arise.

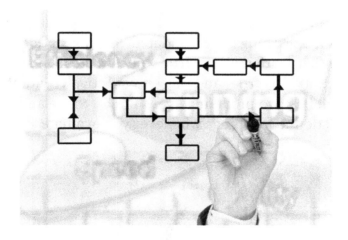

There are two major aspects of control flow: 'conditionals' and 'loops.' Loops are actually built on top of conditionals in a manner of speaking, so we're going to talk about conditionals first. However, both conditionals and loops are built upon the same basic idea that one data set may be compared against another to determine whether a given statement is true. This goes hand in hand with that Bool thing that we were talking about earlier, so we're going to go ahead and talk about boolean values first.

Booleans are relatively easy to understand. As we covered earlier in the book, booleans essentially refer to whether something is true or false. It also means by extension that a boolean value can only ever be true or false and never anything else.

Booleans go far back, and in many ways, the specific implementation of Booleans in PowerShell actually somewhat mimics these older boolean systems that hail from the time of C and Fortran. Back then, booleans were actually integers, stored as either a 0 or a 1. A '0' would mean false, and a '1' would mean true. This system is kept in PowerShell under the hood. Although things are validated as true or false on the surface, underneath it all the true values correspond sharply to a 1 and a 0 for true and false respectively. Additionally, PowerShell has two predefined variables — $true and $false — that it will define for things whenever you evaluate statements.

With that out of the way, it's time that we talk about boolean expression. Boolean expressions are pretty easy to understand. Essentially, they are just expressions. Maybe you remember back in middle or high school when you worked on expressions in math, things such as '$x > 7$.' These essentially take the same form. An entire boolean expression actually evaluates to either true or false, as a statement can only really be true or false anyhow.

In PowerShell, there are numerous different operators intended to compare two things to set up boolean expressions. These operators are as follows:

- **-eq**

This operator checks to see whether the two values are equal.

- **-ne**

This operator checks to see whether the two values are not equal.

- **-gt**

This operator checks to see if the left value is greater than the right.

- **-lt**

This operator checks to see if the left value is lesser than the right.

- **-ge**

This operator checks to see if the left value is greater than or equal to the right.

- **-le**

This operator checks to see if the left value is lesser than or equal to the right.

- **-like**

This operator checks to see if two strings are similarly based upon a textual wildcard.

- **-notlike**

This operator checks to see if two strings are not similarly based upon a textual wildcard.

- **-match**

This operator checks to see if one string matches a section of another string.

- **-notmatch**

This operator checks to see if one string does not match a section of another string.

- **-contains**

This operator checks to see if a given value set contains a specific value x.

- **-notcontains**

This operator checks to see if a given value set does not contain a specific value x.

- **-in**

Similar to -contains.

- **-notin**

Similar to '-notcontains.'

As you can see, these aren't terribly difficult to remember, and they're actually straightforward in their description. They're equally straightforward in their usage.

These boolean comparisons form the basis of all logic. The fact is that all decisions that we ever make involve boolean comparisons, often boolean comparisons nested within other boolean comparisons ad infinitum depending upon how important the decision is and how much information we have to work through. This stays relevant all the time, too. For example, the phrase "If I run out of milk, I will go to the store" contains a boolean expression to be checked, whether you realize it or not: Is it true that I've run out of milk? If it is, I will go to the store. If it is not true, I am not going to the store. (This is the simplest form of logic that you'll learn in a discrete mathematics course.)

Your programs, likewise, will often need to make various different decisions based off of any set of variables that may arise. Fortunately, it's very easy to port this method of decision making to any and all of your programs — you do so through an 'if' statement.

What an, 'if' statement does, is check a condition and then execute a block of code if that condition turns out to be true. Here is the syntax for an 'if' statement:

```
if (condition) {

code goes inside

}
```

Let's assume that we wanted to print out, "There are three oranges," if the number of oranges was equal to three. Here's how we would do that.

```
$oranges = 3

if ($oranges -eq 3) {

Write-Output "There are three oranges."

}
```

This alone isn't very impressive. Moreover, it lacks a certain kind of expandability that makes you really able to perform logical operations using a computer. After all, there is no sort of catch-all statement. All that we provide for is the possibility that there are three oranges.

This creates a dichotomy that I like to call 'passive conditionals' and 'active conditionals.' Passive conditionals are conditionals which are by no means forced to execute. Passive conditionals simply evaluate a singular condition. If the condition turns out not to be true, then the entire conditional block is skipped over. If, on the other hand, the condition turns out to be true, the code within is executed, and the code moves on.

There are also 'else' active conditionals. Active conditionals evaluate a singular condition (or more, if you use elseif statements), but they also have a catch-all clause in case nothing proves true. You can set these up with the following syntax. Bear in mind, though, that only the 'if and else' are required. You don't have to evaluate for an 'elseif' statement. The option is merely there for you to use if you would like to.

Here is the structure of a complete conditional, including the elseif statement:

if (condition) {

code goes inside

} elseif (condition) {

code goes inside

} else {

code goes inside

}

Note that the else statement doesn't have a condition to check. This is because it's your catch-all statement. It runs if none of the other conditions being checked are true. Let's say that we wanted to make our oranges program have a condition for whatever happens:

if ($oranges -eq 3) {

Write-Output "There are $oranges oranges!"

} elseif ($oranges -lt 3) {

Write-Output 'There are less than 3 oranges.'

} else {

Write-Output 'There are more than 3 oranges.'

}

You can see, therefore, the logic of this program. First, it checks to see if there are three oranges. If so, then it prints out that there are three oranges. If that weren't true, then it would next evaluate the elseif condition: Is $oranges less than 3? If it is, then it will print out, 'There are less than 3 oranges.'

However, what if neither of these istrue? Well, logically, if there aren't 3 oranges and there aren't less than 3 oranges, clearly the only alternative is that there are in fact more than 3 oranges. Our catch-all statement then fills in for this potential outcome.

The other thing that we need to talk about is loops. Loops are also massively important in the context of both logic and programming, and they're actually a function that you perform relatively consistently without ever even realizing it. Think of it this way, if ever you are trying to do something over and over, then you are looping.

This may not be quite obvious yet but think of it in terms of counting out loud. In your head, you may not consider it looping or even take into consideration the fact that you're doing something over and over. But you are, you're just changing something each time. Think about it, if you count out loud from 1 to 10, you're performing the same basic action each time. You start with a number, then you say that number out loud which involves opening your mouth, vocalizing the sound of that given number, then relaxing your mouth back to a neutral position for the next word, then you increase the number by one in your head and repeat the process over again until you reach 10.

There are two basic kinds of loops in PowerShell scripting that you need to know. These are for loops and while loops. They are functionally different, and both serve their own niche, even though their core functionality of looping over and over until a condition is met remains the same.

The 'for' loop is intended to be an 'iterator' loop. What the for loop does is allow you to define a starting variable, then a condition for which the loop ends, then it allows you to define the way that the starting variable will change each time through the loop, in essence iterating through the loop.

Let's take our '1 through 10' example again. Let's say that we wanted to print out the numbers 1 through 10 to the console. A 'for' loop would make this especially simple. The syntax in a 'for' loop looks like this:

PowerShell

For (iterator variable initialization; loop continue condition; iterator step)

{

code goes inside

}

When the condition for the loop to continue is no longer true, the loop will be finished, and the next snippet of code outside the loop will be executed.

So, let's think about how we would solve our counting problem. By convention, our iterating variable should be called 'i.' (Placeholder variables normally start with the letter i and move forward as needed.) Our condition should be 'i' and is less than or equal to 10; when i is no longer less than or equal to 10, the loop will no longer run. The iteration should be '+1,' so we should use 'i++' to increase by 1 on each loop. We should also print the value of the variable '$i.'

This gives us the following chunk of code:

For ($i = 1; $i -le 10; i++) {

Write-Output "$i"

}

The other kind of loop is a 'while' loop. These loops are often used for carrying something out until a boolean condition is made false; this specific process is known as a 'game' loop because it mimics the way that games will show the same screen over and over until a certain win or loss condition is met.

While loops are much simpler, all of the logic occurs within them. The only thing that they do is repeat a chunk of code over and over, checking to see if the condition is still true on each run through the code. If it is, the code will run again. If it isn't, the code will not.

The syntax for a while loop is like so:

While (condition) {

code goes inside

}

Now, bearing this in mind, we can try to port the other loop to this while loop just to demonstrate how it would work. The logic stays much the same. However, we must define the iterator variable outside the loop and then increment it within the loop. This is how the code would end up looking:

$i = 1

While ($i -le 10) {

Write-Output "$i"

$i++

}

Now, you should have a solid understanding regarding the most important tools within PowerShell scripting. There is a lot more to learn on top of this, but this is the best way possible to get your feet wet and really start to understand the scripting language and the way that everything works around it. Anything beyond this will be relative to whatever projects it is that you're doing.

Also remember, crucially, that you can call *cmdlets* from within your script. That's partially the entire point of writing PowerShell scripts, automating things that you would normally have to type in and allowing the computer to make complex decisions for you based off of on-the-fly variables.

Conclusion

Thank you for making it through to the end of *PowerShell: Best Practices to Excel While Learning PowerShell Programming*, let's hope it was informative and that it was able to provide you with all of the tools you need to achieve your goals whatever it may be.

The next step is to get more practice. There are plenty of online communities geared towards PowerShell scripting, and a lot of fun or useful projects that people have already done utilizing it. That could mean a pretty major difference for you as a programmer.

The difficult part of learning and executing programming isn't learning how to *do* it but actually practicing and building your skill set through constant exploration.

A lot of work has gone into making this book, and it is my earnest goal that I could help you to become a better programmer and get started on the path to writing PowerShell scripts. If I was able to do this, then I'd very much appreciate it if you'd leave an Amazon review.

Thank you, and good luck!